WUT DO I KNOW?

Common Core
Patricia Ann Callahan Morris
Cover: Patricia

ARCHWAY
PUBLISHING

Archway Publishing books may be ordered through booksellers or by contacting:

Archway Publishing
1663 Liberty Drive
Bloomington, IN 47403
www.archwaypublishing.com
1 (888) 242-5904

Interior Image Credit: All illustrations in workbook by: Patricia

ISBN: 978-1-4808-8158-7 (sc)
ISBN: 978-1-4808-8159-4 (e)

Library of Congress Control Number: 2019913868

Print information available on the last page.

Archway Publishing rev. date: 09/17/2019

Contents

Introduction

The title "WUT DO I KNOW?" is used as a *hook*. It captures the attention of the potential audience to the book. Otherwise, the word what in context is *Grammarly* spelled correctly.

This book addresses the important issue of helping children have improved education so that they can better reach their dreams. But it is a difficult journey for many, due to issues related to Common Core Standards and overall challenges in elementary schools. This book's goal is to help overcome some education deficiencies

Acknowledgment

This book is a labor of love. To be excited to share ideas for teaching mathematics and reading for children in elementary school.

It is important to give thanks to family and friends who encourage the writing of the book.

Ryanne helps print the Alphabet to denote the direction of letters both upper and lower cases and keeping everything on track.

Maurice and Reginald sons both inspired the writing the workbook since I retired.

Kai and Maurice were the children I noticed struggling with mathematics and reading issues and benefited from my ideas.

Sondra, a friend, spent time proofreading whenever asked unconditionally.

Others provided constructive criticisms in the development of the workbook: Tjuana, Katrina, Janice, and Yvette.

Lastly, blessed that God provides the ideas to write in the "Golden Years" of my life.

MISSION VOLUME 1

In summary, the children must practice increasing their proficiency in solving additions, subtractions, equations, word problems, and reading for mastery.

Pre-K

In Pre- K, the children learn the Alphabet, numbers, to print, and to count one to twenty by singing. Singing is an excellent strategy for teaching younger children new information. and retention.

In preparation for kindergarten, it is also the beginnings development of proper social skills, sitting still, listening skills and building new friendships.

Kindergarten

Kindergarten – The children will review the Alphabet, count one to fifty and one to one hundred but not yet having obtained mastery, but have improved after Pre-K experience.

The children begin to learn more about matching primary colors, different positions, and other concepts such as: what is more or less, same or different, sort, print, and the spacing of words.

Their development increases to identify letters missing in words, and how to do simple additions & subtractions.

The children begin to build more excellence in solving, addition, and subtractions using different strategies such as the Tens and Ones, Arrays, Tallies, Blocks, and Number Lines. Those visual aids enhance the children ability to new learning skills.

First Grade

First grade the children again review their prior learning of subjects to build an even stronger working knowledge and retention for the higher grade levels.

The children begin to enjoy their challenges to builds their self-esteem and confidence for more subject requirements of elementary school.

Section 1
PRE-K (Preschool)

Purpose:

Pre- K is the first basis foundation we want to build the children's motivation to learning, inspire their full-attention (lessen distractibility) and other contributing factors in which veer changes in their learning ability.

The children will be described in the workbook as Junior Detectives in solving cases related to mathematics and reading knowledge skills.

The approach will be fun-like, using strategies in which broaden their personal knowledge.

It will be the building block for expanding the Junior Detectives necessary foundation in which to increase their self-esteem and confidence for higher learning grades in the elementary school.

In achievement for their mastery their reward a Junior Detective Badge for completion of each section.

Counting Cases

Junior Detective, the upcoming cases will require working in small groups to review the new evidence found during the investigation.

Each group will delegate who will report the results. The secretary will record the results, stamp case closed, and file.

Case 1. Review counting *one* to *five* out-loud.

Print the numbers *one* to *five*.

Case 2. Review counting *one* to *ten* out-loud.

Print the numbers *one* to *ten*.

Case 3. Review counting *one* to *fifteen* out-loud.

Print the numbers one to *fifteen*.

Case 4. Review counting *one* to *twenty* out-loud.

Print the numbers *one* to *twenty*.

Upon completion of section, receive the Junior Detective Badge.

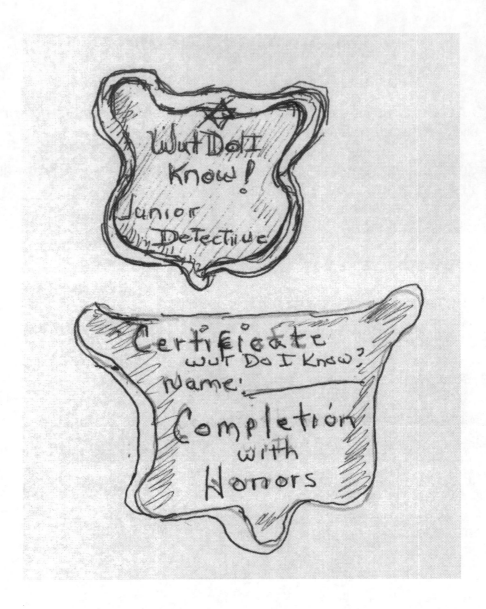

Cars

Bears

owl

puppies

turtles

Quiz: Lesson One Counting.

Case 1. Out-loud recite *five* numbers

Print *five* numbers.

Case 2. What number comes after *eight*?

Case 3. What number comes after *five*?

Case 4. Print numbers *one* to *ten*.

Case 5. Out- loud recite *one* to *fifteen*.

Case 6. Draw *ten* balls.

Case 7. Draw *five* apples.

Case 8. Draw *eight* circles.

Case 9. Draw six squares.

Case 10. Draw *two* circles.

Section 2
Basic Colors Recognition

Objective: Teaching of basic colors recognition

Case 1.

Junior Detectives, your case is to match the colors by drawing a line.

blue*
yellow*
orange
purple *
red *
brown *
black *
green*

green* yellow * orange* purple* red* brown*

Case 2. Mixing two colors to reveal new colors.

a. green and yellow c. blue and purple

b. orange and red d. black and brown

Case 3. In mixing the two colors did the color change?

Circle Yes No

Hands and Fingers: Motor Skills

In preparation in learning to print each letter of the Alphabet, you must be familiar with a child's small hand and finger muscles.

The development of a child's fine motor skills requires some preparation in the building of smaller muscles in the hands. Practice exercises with "Play Dough" or rubber bands for strengthen, and the avoidance of cramping during longer period of time of tracing the Alphabet letters initially.

As an registered occupational therapist having thirty-nine years experience as a practitioner, I know that it is imperative for understanding their child's smaller hand and finger muscles development.

The child's hand can tire out more quickly than the larger muscles in arms and legs, so endurance and strength must be built up gradually before the child's dexterity can improve.

The workbook *will provids an opportunity to practice* tracing each letter in the correct directions by arrows for both upper and lower cases in building those smaller hand and finger muscles.

Here are some suggestions to strengthen the small hand and finger muscles of the child during tracing to determine the child's comfort:

- pasting things on paper

- clap hands

- touching fingers

- buttoning and zipping

- knotting and unknotting rope

- building blocks

- twisting tops of lids

- coloring and drawing

- brushing teeth

- pick up coins and stacking

The Alphabet in Footprints

Junior Detectives, the footprints are drawn and you will print each letter of the alphabet inside the footprints.

Parents, allow the student to do the task. Having the opportunity for self-correction is a major building of their self-esteem and confidence. *They will think I did it.*

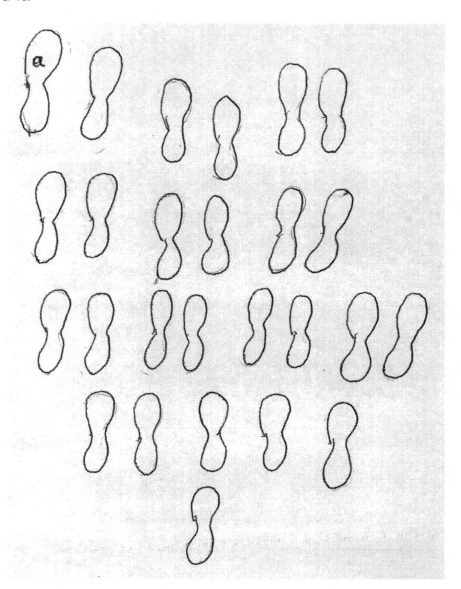

Section 3

Counting and Matching
Different Breeds of Dogs

Junior Detectives, let us take a field trip around the old neighborhood and match the dogs in this case.

Dogs come in different sizes and shapes and even have different personalities just like human beings.

We will take a field trip to see all the different breeds of dogs on our field trip and matching them correctly.

Instructions: Draw lines to match.

Section 4
Sight Word

Instructions:

Begin with three to six letter words.

Junior Detectives, look in papers, books, and other printed materials for three to six letter words. Then paste them on a colorful piece of construction paper and say them out – loud.

Parents the children can make their own favorite words such as their own names, pets or friends for more interest and motivation in learning.

Short Stories

Introducing the younger children to words by drawing and writing their own fantastic adventures.

Junior Detectives, write your own story with the sight words. You can have a parent to help you. Example: Write about an animal, favorite toy, car, trip, building a tree house, best friend, or any imaginary ideal.

Section 5
The Basic Shapes

Junior Detectives, your next case is drawing the basic shapes and thinking where do you see these shapes in your neighborhoods. Parents you can help.

Instructions: Look for the different shapes in the neighborhood and learn what each of these shapes says.

Junior Detectives, draw the four basic shapes. Then tell where you found them in your neighborhood and what does it say.

Square

Rectangle

Circle

Triangle

Quiz: Lesson two Colors

1. Say out-loud the *eight* basic colors.

2. Print the basic *eight* colors.

3.How many basic colors do you know?

4.What your favorite *two* colors?

5.What color is the sky?

6. Print *six* letters of the alphabet.

7.Print *eight* letters of the Alphabet.

8.Print the letters in your first name.

9.What are the basic shapes?

10.Draw *four* basic shapes.

PRE-K
Summation

In Pre-K, the children will begin to learn how to act appropriately and communicate with his or her new environment. The workbook objective is to jump-start this process and ensure he or she develops their ability to stay focused and listen before entering the Kindergarten.

These skills will be necessary in building their foundation for progression in learning for the higher grades.

It will build the children social awareness as well. They learn to work independently or in a group setting. It will instill the child's understanding of other's customs and more respect of differences.

It is a positive way to the build awareness, respect, and future friendships.

The children will be facing new situations. n their development for transition being in a familiar environment into the new and unknown environment but a safe experience.

The advantage of having children to read aloud is to correct any mispronounced words, skipping of words being puzzled about how to say them also understanding, focusing, or unfocused reader, lack of trying or giving up, or refusal to read.

Read aloud fun books from the neighborhood library make an album of special family trips, or special friend.

Take the children to the neighborhood library. There are many good books on their reading levels. Let them read and tell what they have learned. Make a date for reading and going out for treats after their accomplishments.

Every week, bring a new word for the family group to learn write the definition of the word, and then put it in a sentence.

Junior Detectives will earn Junior Detective Badge at completion of section.

Section 6
Kindergarten

A class to prepare the children for First Grade.

"I am going to Kindergarten", Brooklyn G.

Counting

Welcome, Junior Detectives.

Commander Callahan welcomes all the Junior Detectives to the Squad Situation Room.

Commander Callahan will assign the cases weekly.

The skills learned in Pre-K are the first building block in building strong foundation toward the abundance of new learning adventures.

Syllabus

Junior Detectives will learn the following:

1. Learn to count one to fifty and one to hundred.

2. Learn to match basic colors.

3. Learn basic addition.

4. Build vocabulary with new words.

5. Learn the different positions.

6. Learn how to use non-traditional tools to measure.

7. Learn what is fewer or more.

8. Learn how to sort objects by groups of tens.

9. Learn what same or difference means.

10. Learn the five Senses.

11. Learn sight words make new words, adding prefix, and suffix into making new words.

12. Learn to print.

Count

Case 1.

1. Print one to twenty five, one to fifty, one to seventy five, and one to one hundred.

2. Group sets in two, four, six, eight, and ten.

3. Mix colors and identify the new color.

Example: Red and yellow. What is the new shade?

Junior Detectives, the next cases will help you to learn how to process information and solve. Please work independently before asking for assistance.

Case 2. Learn Basic Addition Counting by Ones and Twos Cases.

Example: $1 + 0 = 1$, $1 + 1 = 2$, $1 + 2 = 3$.

$2 + 0 = 2$, $2 + 1 = 3$, $2 + 2 = 4$.

Case 3.

Building Vocabulary with Sight Words

2. Sight Words: fast, go, stop, store, pick, run, fun, meet, food, drink, seen, sister, brother, school, teacher, hair, clothes, shoes, coat, glove, boot, rain, hot, cold, door window, car house, Mc Donald, Wal-Mart's, Wendy, Burger King, grandmother, church, grandfather, church, boat, water, hill, sale, road, bat, ball, cat, and treetop.

Case 4 Developing the children early mental processing skills.

The Junior Detectives will learn to solve different positions cases. Please, read the cases carefully, and circle the best answer.

Positions: Up or Down, Right or Left, The Number, and Inside or Outside.

Case 5. Up or Down.

The mailman notices _six_ mailboxes are down on the lawns with latches opened.

He returns to mail truck for tools to fix the mailboxes.

1. What position did the mailman find the _six_ mailboxes?

Circle the answer. Up or Down

Case 6. Right or Left.

Home For Sale Sign on the lawn for potential buyers. Home location is on the right of Hamilton Subdivision.

Circle the answer. Left or Right

Case 7. What position are the group members in line for the Star Theatre?

The line is long, but everyone in the group decides to stay in line:

Paulette is 5ᵗʰ in line, Roxanne 3ʳᵈ, Margaret 7ᵗʰ, Bobby 4ᵗʰ, Charles 2ⁿᵈ, Maurice 6ᵗʰ, Chester 8ᵗʰ, and Walter 1ˢᵗ in line.

Junior Detectives place each person in the correct **order** by name.

Case 8 Fewer or More Concepts.

Junior Detectives the case assignment is the understanding what is fewer or more in numerals.

Underline answer.

25 - 45 Fewer or More?

75 - 25 Fewer or More?

20 - 10 Fewer or More?

50 - 60 Fewer or More?

80 - 10 Fewer or More?

15 - 12 Fewer or More?

90 - 30 Fewer or More?

55 - 54 Fewer or More?

Case 9. inside or Out.

Underline answer.

1.Garage is inside or outside?

2.Sofa is inside or outside?

3.Bedroom is inside or outside?

4.Pond is inside or outside?

5.Dinning room is inside or outside?

6.Kitchen stove is inside or outside?

7.Bar – B- Q Grill is inside outside?

8.Car is inside outside?

Answer Key

Case 2. Learn Basic Addition Ones and Twos.

Ones

1 + 0 =1

1 + 1= 2

1+ 2 = 3

1+ 3 = 4

1+4 = 5

1+ 5 = 6

1+ 6 = 7

1+ 7 = 8

1+ 8 = 9

1+ 9 = 10

1+10= 11 Got it!

Twos

2 +0 =2

2 +1 =3

2+ 2 =4

2+ 3= 5

2+ 4 =6

2+ 5 =7

2+6 = 8

2+ 7= 9

2+8 =10

2+9 =11

2+10=12 Got it!

Case 6. down

Case 7. right

Case 8. Walter, Charles, Roxanne, Bobby, Palette, Maurice, Margaret, and Chester.

Case 9. fewer, more, more, more, more, more, more, more,

Case 10. outside, inside, inside, outside, inside, inside, outside, outside.

First Grade

Junior Detectives entering into First Grade is the most exciting adventure. The classroom is set up with one to two teachers.

The studies will include reading, writing, math, science, and social

In Wut Do I Know? workbook address only math and reading subjects.

Matching

In matching activity it is important to determine a child's learning styles. There are three types of learning styles:

1.Visual Learner: prefer seeing pictures.

2.Auditory Learner: prefer hear the information.

3.Kinesthetic Learner: prefer "hand-on and "engage in the activity to grasp a concept.

There are techniques to determine a child's concentration and focus:

1. Divide tasks into small or bigger for completion.

2. What is the child's attention- span? Is the child easily distracted?

3. Understanding the child's learning style (visual, auditory, kinesthetic).

In the workbook, it will address all these concerns using visualization, visual memory, active reading, dividing tasks from smaller cases to cases with more detail, and keeping in mind always the different learning styles of children.

The ultimate goal is realizing learning is magical through play. Reading and solving are the rewards for building knowledge. It helps in higher grade levels.

Junior Detectives, the first case will be matching, colors, and shapes.

Look around the house for old magazines and cut out what matches.

Match Color Cases

Case 1.

Draw a line to match the colors below.

Blue

Yellow

Orange

Purple

Red

Brown

Black

Green

Green Brown Purple Black Orange Yellow Red Blue

Case 2. The Junior Detectives will explore colors mixing and see the vast arrays of new colors.

Practice mixing different colors combinations and noticing the different arrays of beautiful color combinations.

Case 3

Make a puzzle and paste on a construction paper

Case 4 Matching by drawing a line.

1.Peanut butter

2.Ham

3.Hot dog

4.Cookies

5,Bacon

6. Catsup

7.Ball

bat, eggs, bun, ice-cream, lettuce, catsup, jelly, mustard

Solving for How Many

Case 1. Group by 10

Solving for 10 sets.

Find small toys to practice grouping by10.

Case 2. Solve how many 2?

1. How many 2 in 4?

2. How many 2 in 8?

3. How many 2 in10?

Case 3 Solve how many 5?

1. How many 5 in 10?

2. How many 5 in 15?

3. How many 5 in 20?

Case 4 Solve how Many 10?

1.How many 10 in 20?

2.How many 10 in 30?

3.How many 10 in 40?

Solving for Positions

Case 5.

Right or Left

1. Print the numbers on the left_____ 2 or 1

2. Up or Down –A. Draw a cup down. B. Draw a boat up

3. **Top or Bottom** - Draw a flowerpot under the table.

4. Bottom or Top- Draw a teddy bear on top of table.

5. Inside or Out - A barn is inside or outside? _____

6. Front and Back A car trunk is front or back? _____

Solving for Same or Difference

Case 6

Underline answers

Example: 5 and 4. Same of <u>Difference</u>

1. Cars and Boat? Same or difference?

2 House and Church? Same or difference?

3. Men and Women? Same or difference?

4. Books and Pencil? Same or difference?

5. Planes and Car? Same or difference?

6. Chairs and Cup? Same or difference?

7. Doors and Refrigerator? Same or difference?

8. Clocks and Book? Same or difference?

9. Beds and House? Same or difference?

10.Book and Lamp? Same or difference?

Answer Key

How Many Cases 2s?

Case 1. 2, 4, 5.

How many 5s?

Case 2. 2, 3, 4.

How many 10s?

Case 3. 2, 3, 4.

Right and left

Positions

Case 4. 2, bottom, top, outside, back.

Same or Difference

Case 5. difference, difference, same, same, same, same, difference, same, same same.

Case 6. Matching

1.Peanut butter - jelly

2. Ham - eggs

3. Hot dog- bun

4. Cookies – ice cream

5. Bacon- eggs

6. Catsup -mustard

7. Ball -bat

Language

Junior Detective your new cases will be **three** letter words to help you read short stories

1. But

2. Dog

3. Cat

4. Man

5. Boy

6. Her

7. Him

8. Why

9. Say

10. Dad

11. Mom

12. Had

13. Out

14. Pat

15. Net

Junior Detective new four letter words to help you read short stories

1. Game	17. Girl
2. More	18. Hook
3. Book	19. Take
4. Fish	20. Five

5. Door   21. Test

6 Long   22. Zero

7.Show   23. Cake

8.Boat   24. Bear

9.Coat   25. Meal

10.Rain

11.Than

12.Blue

13.Word

14.Many

15. Goat

16. Meal

Quiz: Lesson three Language

1. How many three letters words can you recite?

2. How many four letters words can you recite?

3. Draw a object upside down

4. Draw a object on the right side

5. Draw an object on the left side

6. Draw an object outside

7. Draw an object inside

8. How many three letter words can you print?

9. How many four-letter words can up print?

10. Can you print the letters in your first name?

11. Group five objects in a circle

12. Group ten objects in a box.

13. Group fifteen objects in a square.

14. Group twenty objects in a box.

Reading Short Stories

Junior Detectives, reading out loud the three shorts stories cases.

Jamie and Bobby

Jamie and Bobby like to sit on the porch and watch the birds drinking water from the water fountain.

The birds are different color and sizes.

The giant bird keeps the smaller birds away when they are drinking.

and then fly and sit on the white fence to sleep

Bird Houses

Our neighborhood has many different styles, colors, and sizes of the birdhouse in the backyards.

My friends and I like to go and look at each of them and decide which is pretty and which is not so beautiful.

It is our favorite things to do in the neighborhood. Does your community have a birdhouse?

Houseboats

I found a video about houseboats.

The video shows the different styles each person designed their family houseboats. They live on the water.

One houseboat the father designed vertically to accommodate a family of nine.

It is amazing. The first level had all the controls to operate the boat when choosing a different location.

The second level had the kitchen, bedroom, bathroom, and seating areas for the family. The top-level was the area for sunbathing and family gathering.

Other houseboats are not so fabulous as the first one but essential for family in China. Their boats are much smaller, and family sleeps, prepare food band cook. All important activities outside the houseboat are on land.

Have you ever seen a houseboat?

First Grade

Situtation Room

COMPUTATIONS

NUMBER LINE ADDITION CASE

Junior Detectives practice writing the answers in number line form.

1. 10 + 5 =

2 9 + 4 =

3. 8 + 5 =

4. 10 + 4 =

5. 11 + 2 =

6. 6 + 8 =

7. 5 + 6 =

8. 9 + 6 =

9. 15 = +4 =

10. 12 + 3 =

NUMBER LINE SUBTRACTION CASES

Junior Detectives practice writing answers in number line form.

1. 3 – 2 =

2. 13 – 2=

3. 20 - 4 =

4. 38 – 5 =

5. 33 – 8 =

6. 13 - 2 =

7. 7 – 4 =

8. 9 – 6 =

9. 15 -1 =

10. 13 – 9 =

Additions

Junior Detective, the next cases will require you to learn a new strategy in numbers in preparation to process at concrete level and progression into to pre-operational thinking skills.

Let us open a case together before you will be assigned your own cases to solve.

Example: 5 10 + 10= 20.

Case 1.

Detective here are your cases

1.21 + 10 =

2.91 + 10 =

3.72 + 10 =

4.85 + 10 =

5.107+10 =

6.38 + 10 =

7.57 + 10 =

8.25 + 10=

9.103 +10=

10.15 +10 =

11.18 + 10 =

12.9 + 10=

13.106 + 10 =

14.66 + 10 =

15.77 + 10 =

16.88 + 10 =

17.99 +10 =

18.59 +10 + 10=

19.64 + 10 =

20.102 +10=

Answer Key

Case 1.

1.21 + 10 = <u>31</u>

2.91 + 10 = <u>101</u>

3.72 + 10 = <u>82</u>

4.85 + 10 = <u>95</u>

5.107+10 = <u>117</u>

6.38 + 10 = <u>48</u>

7.57 + 10 = <u>67</u>

8.25 + 10= <u>35</u>

9.103 +10= <u>113</u>

10. 15 +10 = <u>25</u>

11. 18 + 10 = <u>28</u>

12. 9 + 10= <u>19</u>

13. 106 + 10 = <u>116</u>

14. 66 + 10 = <u>76</u>

15. 77 + 10 <u>= 87</u>

16. 88 + 10 = <u>98</u>

17. 99 +10 = <u>109</u>

18. 59 + 10 + 10 = <u>69</u>

19. 64 + 10 = <u>74</u>

20 102 +10= <u>102</u>

Subtraction

Junior Detective, your next assignment is solving subtraction.

The memory of numbers is in the parietal lobe-spatial of concrete, operational and development into abstract thinking ability.

Example: 113 - 10 = <u>103</u>

Junior Detective your assignment is to solve these cases.

Case 2.

94 – 10

106 –10

102 - 10

93 – 10

85 – 10

38 – 10

19 - 10

14- 10

11- 10

12- 10

70- 10

114 – 10

116 - 10

111- 10

66 - 10

37 – 10

15.41 – 10

16.91 – 10

17. 54 – 10

18. 10 - 10

Answer Key

Case 2.

1. 84

2. 96

3. 92

4. 83

5. 75

6. 28

7. 9

8. 4

9. 1

10. 2

11. 6

12. 104

13. 106

14. 101

15. 56

16. 27

17. 31

18. 81

19. 44

20. 0

Exponents

One of a set of rules in algebra: exponents of numbers are added when the numbers are multiplied, subtracted when the numbers are divided, and multiplied when raised by still another exponent: 10^2,

5^2, 9^2, addition, subtraction, and multiplication.

Junior Detective, let us solve addition, exponents, subtraction and multiplication for the next cases.

Junior Detective, be careful using the correct signs in solving the cases.

Case 1.

Addition

1. $5^2 + 6 =$

2. $10^2 + 4 = -$

3. $4^{3} + 2 =$

4. $6^3 + 7 =$

5. $2^2 + 1 =$

Case 2.

Subtract

1. $10^2 - 6 =$

2. $9^2 - 3 =$

3. $3^2 - 2 =$

4. $8^2 - 4 =$

5. $7^2 - 3 =$

Case 3

Multiply

1. $10^2 \times 4 =$

2. $2^2 \times 5 =$

3. $7^2 \times 3 =$

4. $6^2 \times 2 =$

5. $9^2 \times 2 =$

Quiz: Lesson four Addition, Subtract, Multiply, and Exponents

Junior Detectives, you have had the opportunity to solve different cases using strategies for subtraction, addition, exponent, and multiplication by 10 problems.

Show work with pictures in tens and ones, blocks, tallies, group 10, words, numbers line, numerals, or spell-out.

Case 1. Subtraction

    1. 54 – 10 =

    2. 95 – 10 =

    3. 112- 10 =

    4. 43 – 10 =

    5. 34 – 10 =

Case 2. Addition

    1. 54 + 10 =

    2. 95 + 10 =

    3. 112+ 10 =

    4. 43 + 10 =

Patricia Ann Callahan Morris

5. 34 + 10 =

Case 3. Number Line Addition and Subtraction.

Solve drawing number line five cases.

1.5 + 10 =

2. 6 + 3 =

3. 4 + 9 =

4. 5 - 3 =

5 .8 - 4 =

6. 10 – 8 =

7. 20 – 10 =

8. 20 - 5

9. 15 – 6 =

10. 10 – 7 =

Case 4. Print sums in number form.

Example: 20 (twenty).

   1. 54 – 10 = <u>40</u>

   2. 95 – 10 = <u>80</u>

   3. 112- 10 = <u>102</u>

   4. 43 – 10 = <u>33</u>

   5. 34 – 10 = <u>24</u>

Answer Key

Case 1 Subtraction one to five.

1. 44

2.85

3.102

4.33

5.24

Case 2 Addition one to five.

1.64

2.105

3.122

4.53

5.44

Case 3 . Number Line one to ten.

1.15

2.9

3.13

4.2

5.4

6.2

7.10

8.15

9.9

10.2

Case 4. **Print in number form one to five.**

1.forty

2.eighty

3.one hundred two

4. thirty three

5. twenty four

Case 1-3 . **Exponents Addition one to five.**

1. 16

2. 24

3. 14

4. 25

5 5

Subtraction one to five.

1. 14

2. 15

3. 4

4. 12

5.11

Exponents Multiplication one to five.

1.80

2. 50

3.42

4.24

5.36

Word Problems

Junior Detectives, three essential tips to understanding how to solve mathematical problems:

1.Assuming what the operation can be in the wording of the question by asking: How many? How many left?

2.The alignment of numerals for addition, subtraction, and multiplication problems for solving.

3. The cases are solving for both addition and subtraction using an innovated strategy such as dominoes as a tool counting the dots.

Show work.

Case 1.

Patricia's dog, the Gangster, hides his four toys under things.

Maurice finds only one toy under the couch. How many Gangster's toys are left? _____

2. Kai tosses five balls to Gangster and Mr. Buttons to catch. She rolls five more balls. How many balls does Kai throw to the dogs? _____

Case 2.

1. Sally is playing with six dolls on her bed with Carmen. She gives her

friend Carmen two babies. How many babies does have Sally left? _____

2. Janice is preparing weekly grocery for market tomorrow.

She needs two loaves of bread, one gallon of milk, two-pack of bacon, one pack of turkey lunchmeat, one lettuce, one package the vine tomatoes, one bottle of French Dressing, one bottle of spaghetti sauce, and one container of medium size paper plates.

How many items on Janice's market list? _____

3, School is out for Spring Break one week. The teacher is assigning the students to read two books, write one paper, and bring to class on Monday.

How many books does the teacher assigned the students to read and to write paper?

Quiz: Lesson five Strategies in drawings to solve mathematical problems.

Junior Detective, what are ways we can draw addition and subtraction problems? Tens and Ones, Tallies, Blocks, and Group of 10.

Detective makes your cases.

Answer Key

Word Problems Cases

Case 1. three left

2. ten balls

Case 2. 1. four baby dolls left

2. eleven items on grocery list

Case 3. 1.2 books

Greater Than Or less Than, Same or Equal

Detective your next cases will be greater than or less than be careful and same or equal to solve.

Instructions: 1. Signs for (>), (<) greater or less.

Numbers greater than cases.

1. 9 - 2

2. 4 - 7

3. 5 - 2

4. 6 - 1

5. 10 - 2

6. 12 - 10

7. 15 - 3

8. 6 - 7

7. 9 - 12

8 8 - 10

9. 15 - 4

10. 2 = 3

Numbers less than cases

1. 3 - 2

2. 4 - 1

3. 6- 7

4. 9- 2

5. 4- 5

6. 1 - 0

7. 5 - 1

8. 1- 3

9. 1 - 12

10. 1- 8

Circle **numbers that are same and equal underline cases**.

1. 5 - 5

2. 3 - 9

3. 6 - 6

4. 2 - 7

5. 8 - 8

6. 7 - 7

7. 4 - 1

8. 15 - 15

9. 20 - 20

10. 11- 11

Answer Key: Greater Than or Less Than, Same and Equal

Greater Than Cases.

1. 9 **(>)**

2. 7**(>)**

3. 5 **(>)**

4. 6 **(>)**

5. 10 **(>)**

6. 12 **(>)**

7. 15 **(>)**

8. 7**(>)**

7. 12**(>)**

8. 10 **(>)**

9. 15 **(>)**

10. 3 **(>)**

(<), signs numbers less than Cases.

1. 3 2(>)

2. 4 1**(>)**

3. 6 7(<)

4. 9 2**(>)**

5. 4 5(<)

6. 1 0**(>)**

7. 5 1**(>)**

8. 1 3(<)

9. 1 12(<)

10. 1 8(<)

Circle the numbers that are same cases and Underline equal cases.

1. 5 5

2. 3 9

3. 6 6

4. 2 7

5. 8 8

6. 7 7

7. 4 1

8. 15 15

9. 20 20

10. 11 11

Fact Family

Detectives the cases will become more challenging in learning group comparison of numbers adding and subtracting in " Fact Family" cases.

When you are learning how to do "Fact Family" addition and subtraction, it can be confusing at first, and then a lot of fun with practice to master. It is basely **related facts** to add and subtract.

Junior Detectives, always remember the order of operation, add, and subtract to solving the correct answers.

Triangle Strategy

It can be solved using the symbol "triangle". A triangle has three sides and vertices.

There are three numbers placed inside the triangle.

Step 1. Add the two bottom numbers (right to left numbers).

Step 2. Add the two bottom numbers (left to right numbers).

Step 3. Subtract the top number with the bottom number (right

number).

Step 4: Subtract the top number with the bottom number (left figure),

Horizontal Position Strategy

Example: Horizontal position.

2 + 3 = 5, 5 - 2 = 3

3 + 2 = 5 5 – 3 = 2

The top number in the problem is 12.

Step 1. Add 5 + 7 = <u>12</u>

Step 2. Add 7 + 5 = <u>12</u>

Step 3. 12- 7 = <u>5</u>

Step 4. 12 − 5 = <u>7</u>

Fact Family Cases

Option: Either approachs is appropriate but it is encouraged to practice both to master.

1. 10, 5, 5

2. 15, 7, 8

3. 13, 4, 9

4. 7,2, 9,

Junior Detectives, practice making cases using both approaches to master related facts of "Fact Family".

Answer Key

Fact Family Cases

1.. 5 + 5 = 10 10 - 5 = 5

5 +5 = 10 10 - 5 = 5

2. 8 + 7 = 15 15- 8 = 7

7 = 8 = 15 15- 7 = 8

3. 9 + 4 = 13 13 – 9 = 4

4 + 9 = 13 13 – 4 = 9

4. 7 + 2 = 9 9 – 7 = 2

2 + 7 = 9 9 – 2 = 7

Missing Numbers

Example: 1 2 3 _____ 5 6 7 8 9 10. Completed Sequence: 1 2 3 4 5 6 7 8 910.

1. 11 12 13 14 15 16 17 20

2. 21 22 23 24 27 28 29 30.

3. 31 32 33 34 35 36 37 38 39

4. 41 42 43 4 4 45 46 50

Write the complete sequence up to 100.

5. 51 52 53 54 55 56 60.

6. 61 62 63 64 65 66 67 68 69.

7. 71 72 73 74 76 77 78 79 80.

8. 82 83 84 85 86 90

9. 91 92 93 94 95 98 99 100.

Answer Key Missing Numbers

1 2 3 4 5 6 7 8 9 10 11 12 13 14 15 16 17 18 19 20 21 2223242526 27 28 29 30 31 32 33 34 35 36 37 38 39 40 41 42 43 44 45 46 47 48 4 9 50 51 52 53 54 55 56 57 58 59 60 61 62 63 64 65 66 67 68 69 70 71 72 73 74 75 76 77 78 79 80 8182 83 84 85 86 87 88 89 90 91 92 93 94 95 96 97 98 99 100

Ten-Frame Strategy for Addition and Subtraction

Detective's tools

This case is on "Ten-Frame" addition and subtraction. The report needs to be on Captain Morris 'desk before noon.

Check all the facts before submitting your reports. The captain does not like any mistakes when reporting to the community the problem(s) case solved by his detectives.

*Detectives make your own Ten-Frame Mat is solving the addition and subtraction problems. Show your work.

1. 6 + 7 =

2. 8 + 9 =

3. 10 + 2 =

4. 3 + 9 =

5. 9 - 3 =

6. 10 - 4 =

Now, the detective starts writing your problems and solving them until mastery; this is the ultimate goal in these case assignments.

Answer Key Ten- Frames

1. 6+7 = 13

2. 8+9 = 17

3. 10+2 = 12

4. 3 + 9= 12

5. 9-3 = 6,

6 5. 10-4 = 6

Telling Time - Hour

Detective the cases in telling time by the hours and half hours.

Example: Draw a clock -Time 7:00

Draw The Clocks

Hours

7:00 1:00 3:00 5:00

10:00 11:00 12:00 2:00

What time do you get up? Draw a clock with the time you get up.

Telling Time – Half- Hour

Detective the cases will be telling time half hours.

Example: Draw the clock for 7:30.

7:30 12:30 1:30 6:30

9:30 2:30 4:30 5:30

1. What time do you go to bed? Draw the clock.

Non- Traditional Measurements

There are many ways to teach about measurements for a first grader. We will explore some of those ways.

Junior Detective, we will begin this adventure in solving together. Are you ready to have fun exploring with non-measuring tools?

Instructions: Tools to use in measuring a straight line:

- paper clips

- coins

- cubes

- cars

- pencils

- string and others objects.

- brushes

- coins

- rubber bands

Word Problems

Word problems can be hard due to not reading them carefully, and understanding what the story is asking to be solved.

Junior Detectives, keep in mind when reading the cardinal rule of the Five W's":

Who

What

When

Where

Why

The Family Camping Trip

The family is planning a camping trip for Florida.

Mom says," Kai and Maurice go to be bed early. Dad is planning for us to leave at 10:00 tomorrow in the RV."

Kai starts packing her bag with clothes she wants to take on for the trip, 4 tops, 4 pairs of shorts, 2 bras, 4 pairs of underwear, 1 pair of gym shoes, 1 pair of flip flops, and I cell phone and adapter, 1 toothbrush and 1 tube of toothpaste, 1 comb, and 1 brush.

Maurice is packing his bag as well, four pairs of underwear, four pairs of shorts, four tops, one pair of gym shoes, one pair of flip flops, one jacket, one cell phone, and adapter, one tooth bush, 1 tube of toothpaste, one hair comb, and two favorite trucks.

Mom is packing all the supplies for the trip, four sleeping bags, four blankets, four pillows, one large tent, one small tent, two wicker boxes, ten package foods items, one cooler, two cans of bug spray, four small flashlights, and 1 Emergency Kit.

Mom is packing her and dad's bags with personal items as well, and cell phones with their adapters.

Dad is packing everything tonight in the RV and checking everything before the trip tomorrow.

We arrive safely at the campsite. Mom and dad begin unpacking only the camping supplies and placing into the smaller tent the wicker basket with lids to keep out bugs.

Mom yells, " Our clothes will take in the RV, so when we shower, we can change in the RV, not at the campsite.".

Mom and dad have everything organized, and Mom prepares a light meal for dinner before getting ready to sleep in the tent.

Quiz: Lesson Six Word Problem

1. What items did Kai pack?

2. What things did Maurice pack?

3. What items did mom pack?

4. When did the family plan to leave?

5. What is the family's transportation for traveling to Florida?

6. Who packed the RV?

7. What did dad do the night before leaving?

8. What did mom do first at the campsite?

9. Why did mom use the wicker baskets?

10. What were the reasons mom left the families clothes in RV?

11. Where is the campsite?

Bonus Question

1. What are the total items Kai packed?

2. What are the total things Maurice packed?

3. What two favorite toys packed?

WORD PROBLEM

WORD PROBLEM

Junior Detective, practice a few of your own addition problems to master this strategy for practicing with addition and subtraction. It is a much faster a more straightforward concept in understanding how to add the hundreds, tens, and one's problems. It is called <u>Expansion</u>.

Bonus: Show your work.

346 + 298 =

298 + 584 =

336 + 765 =

421 + 567 =

789 + 345 =

123 + 789 =

754 + 324 =

124 + 978 =

765 + 234 =

10. 218 + 332 =

Answer Key Bonus Problems (Detective Badges)

Bonus: Show your work. Expansion

346 + 298 = 300 + 40 + 6 + 200 + 90 + 8 = <u>644</u>

298 + 584 = 200 + 90 + 8 + 500 + 80 + 4 = <u>882</u>

336 + 765 = 300 = 30 + 6 + 700 + 60 + 5 = <u>1,101</u>

421 + 567 = 400 + 20+ 1 + 500 + 60 + 5 = <u>988</u>

789 + 345 = 700 + 80+ 9 + 300+ 40+ 5 = <u>1,134</u>

789 - 127 =700 – 80- 9 – 100 – 20- 7 = <u>662</u>

754 - 324 =700 – 50- 4 _ 300 – 20- 4 – 300- 20- 4 =<u>430</u>

978 - 124 = 900 – 70- 8 – 100- 20- 4 = <u>854</u>

765 - 234 = 700 -60- 5 – 200 – 30- 4 = <u>531</u>

10. 332- 218 = 300 -30- 2 – 200 – 10 – 8 = <u>124</u>

LANGUAGE

Detective reading is a lot of fun. You will be reading short story cases and answering questions at the end. First let touch bases on parts of a sentence, nouns, pronouns, action verbs, adverbs, adjectives, coordinating conjunctions, prepositions, punctuation, commas, parentheses, semicolons, and capitalization.

Then learn about what is prefixes and suffixes beginning and ends of root words.

The **noun** is a person, place or thing -Mary, Sam, Ronda, Detroit, Georgia, Florida, house, car, boat or building hammer, nail, bags, truck.

Remember you can't say much without nouns.

The pronoun makes the sentence flow. It refers back to the noun instead of repeating what you said. Instead, Patricia says she or her.

Personal pronouns take the place of a specific person, place, or thing.

Example: First person: I, we.

Second person: you.

Third-person: it, she, they.

The action verb is running, playing, talking, riding, carrying, sitting, falling, and tiring.

It describes an action or state of being.

The **adverb** describes how something was done or how it was done firmly, inside, outside, beautifully, carefully, and especially,

Remember adverbs can describe:

How?

Where?

When?

and to what extent?

The **adjective** describes something about the noun Pat is pretty, short, slim, and smart.

The **preposition** from, and, nor, by, or, yet and so. (Analog:I use is fanboys in remembering the prepositions.)

A preposition is a word used to tie a noun or pronoun to other information in a sentence.

The **vowels** are a, e, I, o u.

What is the use of vowels?

"A" is used when a subject starts with consonant letters other than a, e, I, o, u.

In speaking the word **"The"** it is pronounced two different ways. "The" followed after a **vowel** is pronounced "the" and not accompanied by a consonant is declare "the".

Practice pronouncing the word "the" to hear the differences.

Consonants are b, c, d, f, g, h, j, k, l, m, n, p, q, r, s, t, v, w, x, y, and z.

Punctuation is period, common, semicolon, colon, question mark, exclamation point, dash, a hyphen, parentheses, brackets, braces, apostrophe, quotation marks, and ellipsis – 14 total.

Prefix and Suffix

You will learn the beginnings and endings can change the word's meaning.

Commas are slight pause, an opportunity to take in a breath. before you continues in a sentence.

When to use a comma:

- After an introductory phrase or clause.

- With a nonessential clause.

- At a natural pause.

- In a series.

- With two independent clauses and a conjunction.

Parentheses will provide background information. Example: My favorite drink (Vernor) tastes great with my hamburger on a hot afternoon.

Capitalization is the first word in a sentence, proper noun, days of the week, month, and holidays, special events, and proper adjectives.

Let us start an investigation on how word's beginnings and endings together will change the meaning of the root words.

Case: Active

Beginnings of words: **Prefix** is a group of letters placed before the root of a word.

Pre - meaning before

Post - afterward

Re- "again" or "again and again," to indicate repetition, back and backward.

Practice words: Prefix

a. "happy" - "unhappy."

Meanings changed

"joy," "sad."

b. "comfortable "uncomfortable."

enjoying physical discomfort (pain)

Group Activity: Think of words you change the root with a prefix placed at the beginning root word.

Endings of words: A Suffix is a group of letters at the end of a root word.

Practice words: Suffix

a. Rain - raining

b. Luck - luckily

c. Bad - badly

d. Friend - friendly

e. Mean - meaningful

f. Plenty - plentiful

Group Activity: Choose words and change the root word endings.

Junior Detectives, it is a lot to remember about the parts of a sentence but when you read or begin to writing. It is helpful to know the rules in using them correctly for I did not understand grammar when I was younger.

Short Story

THE THUNDERSTORM

The children like to play outside, catching the bright red ball. Then they heard a loud rumble in the sky.

The mom called them to come inside before the rain starts before they get wet.

They decided to read a book grandma brought from the store and sit in a circle on the rug. They could hear the loud thundering as they sat while grandma read to them.

Then later, the sun came out. Grandma let them go back out to play with the big red ball but not to jump in the puddles.

When they looked up into the sky, they saw a big bright rainbow over the house's roof. The colors are beautiful red, blue, yellow, and orange.

They called out to grandma, "Come see the beautiful rainbow over the roof, grandma."

Answer the Questions

1. What did the kids like play outside?

2. What did they hear outside?

3. Where did they go when the rain started?

4. What did they do inside?

5. What did they see when playing outside?

6. Who did they call to see the beautiful rainbow over the roof?

7. Who brought the storybook the children read during the storm?

8. Did the thunder stop and a rainbow appear?

Grandma's Puppies

I help grandma Pat take care of the puppies.

The puppy's names are Mr. Buttons and Mr. Gangster.

I put water in their dish and food in the pan. The puppies drink a lot of water and dog food in a week.

Grandma does not allow the puppies table food.

She says their little digestive systems do process foods like humans. She does not want them to get ill and have to take to them to Vet Hospital.

Grandma let the puppies play inside and outside with their favorite toys.

They both run and jump flipping the toy when grandma throws it. She throws it back and forth up into the air.

Sometimes they bump their bodies against the couch running so fast to catch the toy.

Grandma and I laugh so loudly it sometimes frightens them, and they run and hide under the couch and the large chair to hide.

Then they come out and fall asleep on their soft puppy's beds.

Answer the question.

1. What are the puppy's names?

2. What do the puppies like to do inside the house?

3. What does grandma not allows the puppies to eat?

4. What makes grandma and I laugh so loud?

5. Where does grandma allow the puppies to play?

Buzz and Mr. Buttons Family Trip to Grandma's House

Buzz and Mr. Buttons are going on a trip with the family to grandma's house. Dad packs the car with all the bags and checks the porch before closing the trunk.

Tommy says, " Oh dad, you forgot Mr. Buttons and his favorite toy he likes to play with'. Dad calls out to mom, " Janice brings Mr. Buttons and his girlfriend so we can beat the heavy traffic."

Mom yells back, " Okay," Mr. Buttons and I are coming."

Mom and Mr. Button both get into the car, and dad starts the car and pulls slowly out the driveway and heads for the expressway. Dad says, " The traffic is light now, but it will be heavier in the next few hours."

Mom is quiet reading her book, and Mr. Button is sleeping with his toy by his side. I am so excited about watching the cars and building passing by on the highway. The drive is long, but I am too happy to go to sleep.

Daddy stops to get gas. Mom runs inside to pick up a few treats for her and I to snack on along the way. We get back on the busy highway heading in the direction of grandma home state, Michigan.

We have crossed the Michigan State line and now it only a few more hours we will reach grandma's house. I can remember grandma always has freshly baked goodies and cold lemonade to drink.

Daddy is hoping he can surprise grandma because we arrived much earlier before more substantial traffic on the roadway. He pulls into the driveway, and suddenly, the big door opens, and grandma is standing with her apron and waving.

Daddy could not surprise her once again. She seems always to sense when he is pulling into the driveway. Is grandma psychic?

Daddy decided not to unpack the car now but to go inside and rest. The house smells with pleasant aromas from the kitchen.

Grandma wants all of us to sit down for dinner. Boy was I glad. I was hungry and could hear strange sounds coming from my belly. Mr. Buttons was hungry as well and ate and drank water. He fell asleep by grandma's rocking chair.

It is always great to go visiting grandma and seeing my old playmates in Michigan.

Questions.

1. Why did daddy want to leave early?

2. Who did daddy almost leave?

3. What did mom get from the gas station store?

4. What does grandma bake when we come to visit?

5. What did Buzz like to do when riding on the trip?

6. What did Mr. Buttons do once in the car?

7. Where was his girlfriend?

8. What did mom do riding in the car?

9. Who opens the door when daddy pulled into the driveway?

10. What was grandma wearing?

Printed in the United States
By Bookmasters